Visual Flexbox

Visual Flexbox

Oluwatobi Sofela

C<>DESWEETLY

First published by CodeSweetly 2022

VISUAL FLEXBOX

First published November 2, 2022 as CSS Flexbox Explained Visually

Second edition November 28, 2022.

www.codesweetly.com

Contents

Contents

Important Terms

Flex Container vs. Flex Item

A flex container (the large yellow area) is an HTML element whose display property's value is flex or inline-flex. Flex items (the smaller boxes within the yellow container) are the direct children of a flex container.

Flexbox's Main vs. Cross Axis

A flexbox's main axis is the layout orientation defined by a flex-direction property. Its cross axis is the perpendicular orientation to the main axis.

@oluwatobiss

@codesweetly

codesweetly.com

justify-content

justify-content: flex-start

flex-start aligns a flexible container's items with the main-start side of the flexbox's main axis.

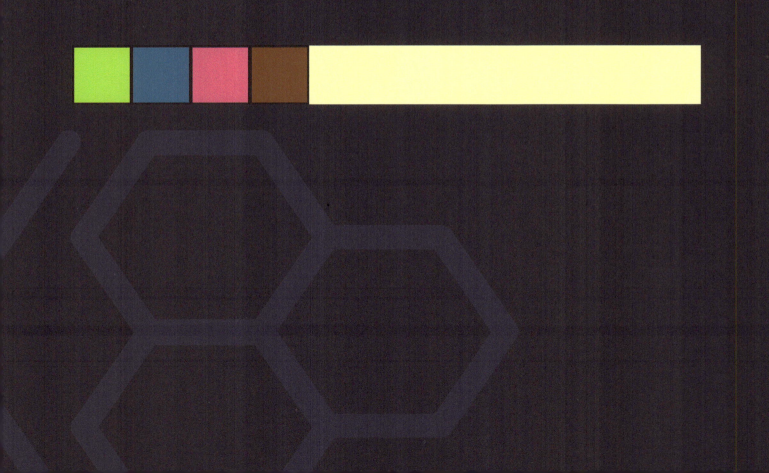

justify-content: center

center aligns a flexible container's items to the center of the flexbox's main axis.

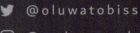

justify-content: flex-end

flex-end aligns a flexible container's items with the main-end side of the flexbox's main axis.

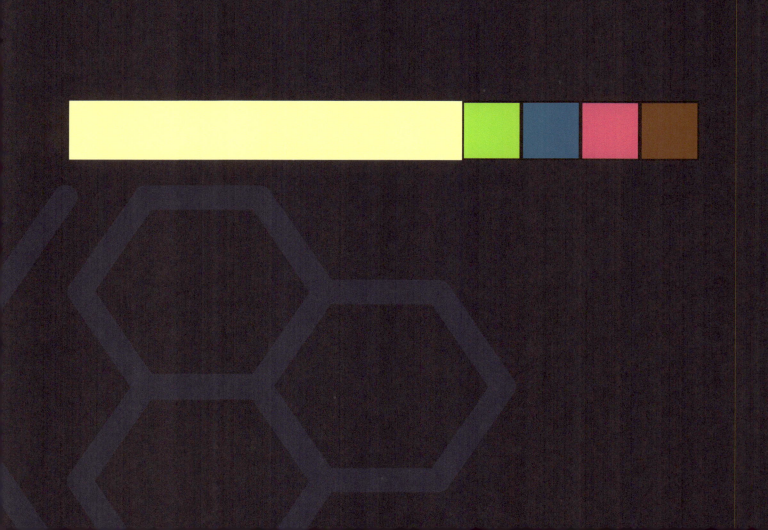

justify-content: space-between

space-between creates even spacing between each pair of items between the first and last item.

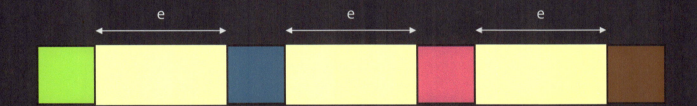

justify-content: space-around

space-around assigns equal spacing to each side of a flexible container's items.

justify-content: space-evenly

space-evenly assigns even spacing to both ends of a flexible container and between its items.

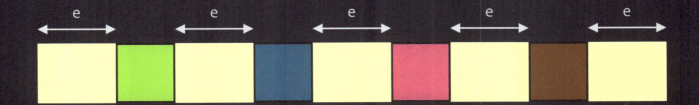

justify-content's Values

flex-start

center

flex-end

space-between

space-around

space-evenly

align-items

align-items: stretch

stretch stretches a flexible container's items to fill the flexbox's cross-axis.

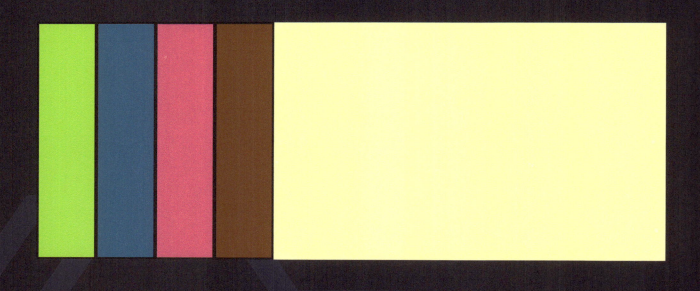

align-items: flex-start

flex-start aligns a flexible container's items with the cross-start edge of the flexbox's cross-axis.

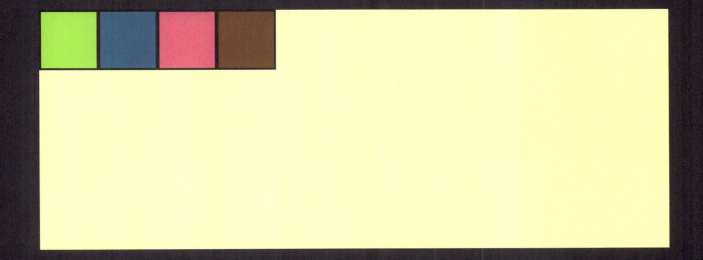

align-items: center

center aligns a flexible container's items to the center of the flexbox's cross-axis.

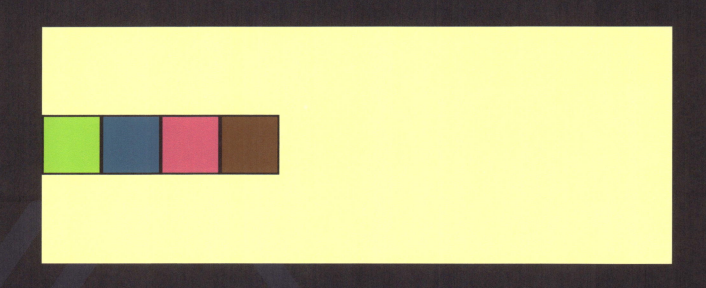

align-items: flex-end

flex-end aligns a flexible container's items with the cross-end edge of the flexbox's cross-axis.

align-items: baseline

baseline aligns a flexible container's items with the baseline of the flexbox's cross-axis.

baseline

align-content

align-content: stretch

stretch stretches the flexible container's lines to fill the flexbox's cross-axis.

align-content: flex-start

flex-start aligns a flexible container's lines with the cross-start edge of the flexbox's cross-axis.

align-content: center

center aligns a flexible container's lines to the center of the flexbox's cross-axis.

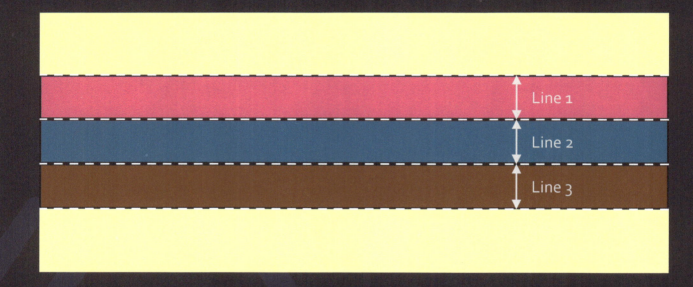

align-content: flex-end

flex-end aligns a flexible container's lines with the cross-end edge of the flexbox's cross-axis.

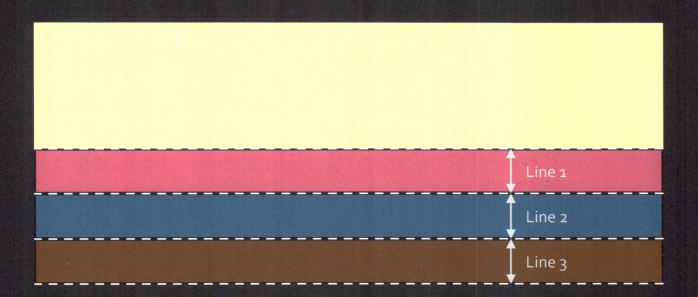

align-content: space-between

space-between creates equal spacing between each pair of lines between the first and last line

align-content: space-around

space-around assigns equal spacing to each side of a flexible container's lines.

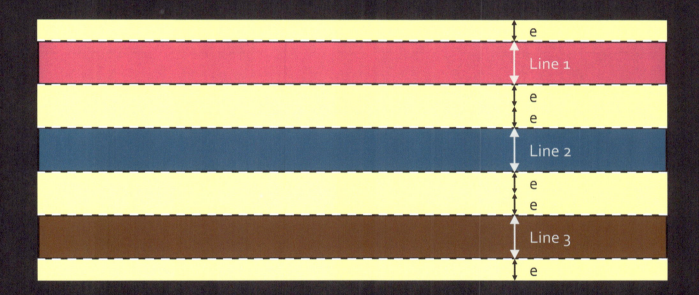

align-content: space-evenly

space-evenly assigns even spacing to both ends of a flexible container and between its lines.

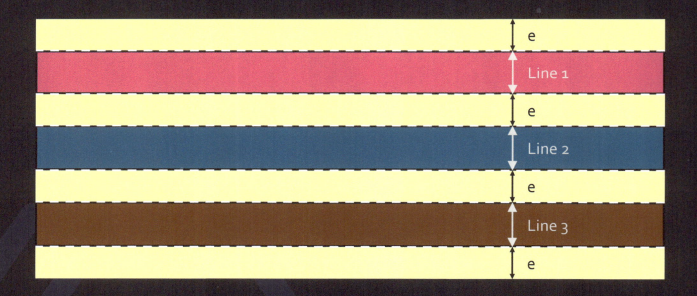

align-self

align-self: stretch

stretch stretches the selected flexible item(s) to fill the flexbox's cross-axis.

align-self: flex-start

flex-start aligns the selected flexible item(s) with the cross-start edge of the flexbox's cross-axis.

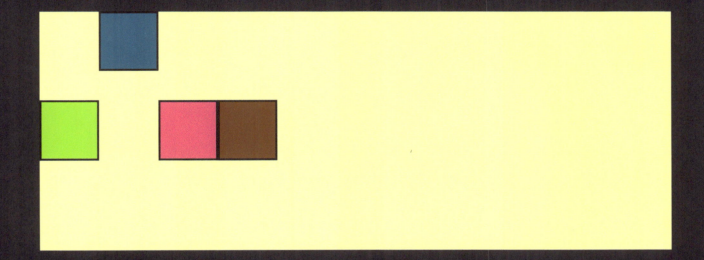

align-self: center

center aligns the selected flexible item(s) to the center of the flexbox's cross-axis.

align-self: flex-end

flex-end aligns the selected flexible item(s) with the cross-end edge of the flexbox's cross-axis.

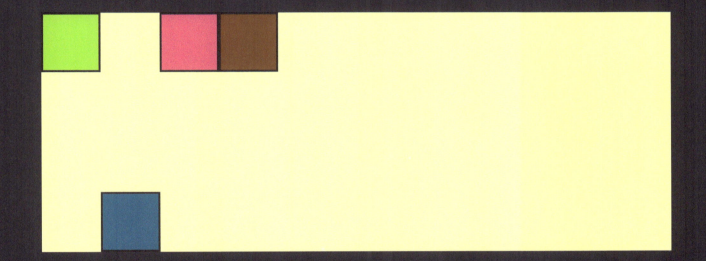

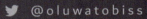
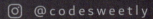

Other CodeSweetly Books...

CSS Flexbox: Complete Guide

Available at Amazon
(https://www.amazon.com/dp/B0BN9DD7QF)

React Explained Clearly

Available at Amazon
(https://www.amazon.com/dp/B09KYGDQYW)

C<8>DESWEETLY

CodeSweetly exists specifically to help make coding so easy and fun to learn.

Visit codesweetly.com to learn web technology topics with simplified articles, images, and cheat sheets.